A word of comfort

COME TO ME

Come to me, all of you who are tired from carrying your heavy loads, and I will give you rest. Take my yoke and put it on you, and learn from me, for I am gentle and humble in spirit; and you will find rest. The yoke I will give you is easy, and the load I will put on you is light.

MATTHEW 11: 28-30

TRUST IN GOD

But I will bless the person
who puts his trust in me.
He is like a tree growing near a stream
and sending out roots to the water.
It is not afraid when hot weather comes,
because its leaves stay green;
it has no worries when there is no rain;
it keeps on bearing fruit.

JEREMIAH 17: 7-8

THE PEACE OF GOD

Don't worry about anything, but in all your prayers ask God for what you need, always asking him with a thankful heart. And God's peace, which is far beyond human understanding, will keep your hearts and minds safe, in Christ Jesus.

PHILIPPIANS 4: 6-7

SURE AS THE SUNRISE

The people say, 'Let's return to the Lord!
He has hurt us, but he will be sure to
heal us;
he has wounded us, but he will bandage our
wounds, won't he?
In two or three days he will revive us,
and we will live in his presence.
Let us try to know the Lord.
He will come to us as surely as the day
dawns,
as surely as the spring rains that water the
earth.'

HOSEA 6: 1-3

HELP IN TROUBLE

Let us give thanks to the God and Father of our Lord Jesus Christ, the merciful Father, the God from whom all help comes! He helps us in all our troubles, so that we are able to help those who have all kinds of troubles, using the same help that we ourselves have received from God. Just as we have a share in Christ's many sufferings, so also through Christ we share in his great help.

2 CORINTHIANS 1: 3-5

STRENGTH RENEWED

Israel, why then do you complain
that the Lord doesn't know your troubles
or care if you suffer injustice?
Don't you know? Haven't you heard?
The Lord is the everlasting God;
he created all the world.
He never grows tired or weary.
No one understands his thoughts.
He strengthens those who are weak and
tired.
Even those who are young grow weak;
young men can fall exhausted.
But those who trust in the Lord for help
will find their strength renewed.
They will rise on wings like eagles;
they will run and not get weary;
they will walk and not grow weak.

ISAIAH 40: 27-31

ALL WE NEED

I prayed to the Lord and he answered me;
he freed me from all my fears.
The oppressed look to him and are glad;
they will never be disappointed.
The helpless call to him, and he answers;
he saves them from all their troubles.
His angel guards those who fear the Lord
and rescues them from danger.

Find out for yourself how good the Lord is!
Happy is the man who finds safety in him!
Fear the Lord, all his people;
those who fear him have all they need . . .

The good man suffers many troubles,
but the Lord saves him from them all.

PSALM 34: 4-9, 19

YOU ARE MINE

Israel, the Lord who created you says,
'Do not be afraid—I will save you.
I have called you by name—you are mine.
When you pass through deep waters,
I will be with you;
your troubles will not overwhelm you.
When you pass through fire, you will not be
burnt;
the hard trials that come will not hurt you.
For I am the Lord your God,
the holy God of Israel, who saves you.

ISAIAH 43: 1-3

GREAT COMPASSION

'I turned away angry for only a moment,
but I will show you my love for ever.'
So says the Lord who saves you.
'In the time of Noah I promised
never again to flood the earth.
Now I promise not to be angry with you
again;
I will not reprimand or punish you.
The mountains and hills may crumble,
but my love for you will never end;
I will keep for ever my promise of peace.'
So says the Lord who loves you.

ISAIAH 54: 8-10

THE GLORY OF THE LORD

'Comfort my people,' says our God.
'Comfort them! Encourage the people of
Jerusalem..
Tell them they have suffered long enough
and their sins are now forgiven.
I have punished them in full for all their
sins.'
A voice cries out,
'Prepare in the wilderness a road for the
Lord!
Clear the way in the desert for our God!
Fill every valley:
level every mountain.
The hills will become a plain,
and the rough country will be made smooth.
Then the glory of the Lord will be revealed,
and all mankind will see it.
The Lord himself has promised this.'

ISAIAH 40: 1-5

GOOD NEWS

Jesus went to Nazareth, where he had been brought up, and on the Sabbath day he went as usual to the synagogue. He stood up to read the Scriptures, and was handed the book of the prophet Isaiah. He unrolled the scroll and found the place where it is written:

'The Spirit of the Lord is upon me.
He has anointed me to preach the Good News to the poor,
He has sent me to proclaim liberty to the captives,
And recovery of sight to the blind,
To set free the oppressed,
To announce the year when the Lord will save his people!'

Jesus rolled up the scroll, gave it back to the attendant, and sat down. All the people in the synagogue had their eyes fixed on him. He began speaking to them: 'This passage of scripture has come true today.'

LUKE 4: 16-21

GOD'S FLOCK

Jerusalem, go up on a high mountain
and proclaim the good news!
Call out with a loud voice, Zion;
announce the good news!
Speak out and do not be afraid.
Tell the towns of Judah
that their God is coming!
The Sovereign Lord is coming to rule
  with power,
bringing with him the people he has
rescued.
He will take care of his flock like a
shepherd;
he will gather the lambs together
and carry them in his arms;
he will gently lead their mothers.

ISAIAH 40: 9-11

THE GOOD SHEPHERD

'I am the good shepherd. The good shepherd is willing to die for the sheep. The hired man, who is not a shepherd and does not own the sheep, leaves them and runs away when he sees a wolf coming; so the wolf snatches the sheep and scatters them. The hired man runs away because he is only a hired man and does not care for the sheep. I am the good shepherd. As the Father knows me and I know the Father, in the same way I know my sheep and they know me. And I am willing to die for them.'

JOHN 10: 11-15

A PLACE PREPARED FOR YOU

'Do not be worried and upset,' Jesus told
them. 'Believe in God, and believe also in
me. There are many rooms in my Father's
house, and I am going to prepare a place for
you. I would not tell you this if it were not
so. And after I go and prepare a place for
you, I will come back and take you to
myself, so that you will be where I am. You
know how to get to the place where I am
going.' Thomas said to him: 'Lord, we do
not know where you are going; how can we
know the way to get there?' Jesus answered
him: 'I am the way, I am the truth, I am the
life; no one goes to the Father except by
me.'

JOHN 14: 1-6

SING PRAISE!

The Lord is a refuge for the oppressed, a place of safety in times of trouble. Those who know you, Lord, will trust you; you do not abandon anyone who comes to you.

Sing praise to the Lord who rules in Zion!
Tell every nation what he has done!
God remembers those who suffer;
he does not forget their cry.

PSALM 9:9-12

GOD'S HAPPY PEOPLE

Happy are those who know they are
spiritually poor: the Kingdom of heaven
belongs to them!
Happy are those who mourn:
God will comfort them!
Happy are the meek:
they will receive what God has promised!
Happy are those whose greatest desire is to
do what God requires:
God will satisfy them fully!
Happy are those who show mercy to others:
God will show mercy to them!
Happy are the pure in heart:
they will see God!
Happy are those who work for peace among
men:
God will call them his sons!

MATTHEW 5: 3-9

NEVER DISCOURAGED

Let us run with determination the race that lies before us. Let us keep our eyes fixed on Jesus, on whom our faith depends from beginning to end. He did not give up because of the cross! On the contrary, because of the joy that was waiting for him, he thought nothing of the disgrace of dying on the cross, and is now seated at the right side of God's throne.

Think of what he went through, how he put up with so much hatred from sinful men! So do not let yourselves become discouraged and give up.

HEBREWS 12: 1-3

'YOUR FATHER IN HEAVEN KNOWS . . .'

Isn't life worth more than food? and isn't the body worth more than clothes? Look at the birds flying around: they do not plant seeds, gather a harvest, and put it in barns; your Father in heaven takes care of them! Aren't you worth much more than birds? . . .

And why worry about clothes? Look how the wild flowers grow: they do not work or make clothes for themselves. But I tell you that not even Solomon, as rich as he was, had clothes as beautiful as one of these flowers. It is God who clothes the wild grass—grass that is here today, gone tomorrow, burned up in the oven. Will he not be all the more sure to clothe you? How little is your faith!

So do not start worrying: 'Where will my food come from? or my drink? or my clothes?' (These are the things the heathen are always after.) Your Father in heaven knows that you need all these things. Instead give first place to his Kingdom and to what he requires, and he will provide you with all these other things.

MATTHEW 6: 25-33

ETERNAL GLORY

We know that God, who raised the Lord
Jesus to life, will also raise us up with Jesus
and bring us, together with you, into his
presence . . .

For this reason we never become
discouraged. Even though our physical
being is gradually decaying, yet our spiritual
being is renewed day after day. And this
small and temporary trouble we suffer will
bring us a tremendous and eternal glory,
much greater than the trouble. For we fix
our attention, not on things that are seen,
but on things that are unseen. What can be
seen lasts only for a time, but what cannot
be seen lasts for ever.

2 CORINTHIANS 4: 14, 16-18

ALL THINGS MADE NEW

Then I saw a new heaven and a new earth. The first heaven and the first earth disappeared, and the sea vanished. And I saw the Holy City, the new Jerusalem, coming down out of heaven from God, prepared and ready, like a bride dressed to meet her husband. I heard a loud voice speaking from the throne: 'Now God's home is with men! He will live with them, and they shall be his people. God himself will be with them, and he will be their God. He will wipe away all tears from their eyes. There will be no more death, no more grief, crying, or pain. The old things have disappeared.'

REVELATION 21: 1-4